The Reality - What Next?

Our Continuing Response

Copyright: October 2024

Tim Sweetman

Scripture references within this book are taken from the The New Living Translation bible unless otherwise noted.

Foreword:

Here is a book that I felt would be helpful for those of us who have encountered Jesus in some way, are now aware of the reality of Him in the now of today and are wondering how we might respond to that reality:
What comes next?

Jesus offers us a door, through which we might enter into His kingdom. A kingdom of life, an eternal kingdom that we might enter today.

I have recently written a short summing up of the life of Jesus on earth: why He came, what He taught, of His victory over death, His resurrection and of His return to heaven, where God dwells.

After these world changing and momentous events, on the day of Pentecost, Holy Spirit came to live in and amongst those who follow Jesus; those who are His disciples.

It was Peter who, with others, gave an explanation to those who watched and experienced the pouring out and manifestation of Holy Spirit amongst them at that time.
We can read about those events in *The Acts of the Apostles chapter two.*

Three thousand people on that occasion, and millions of people since, have followed Jesus and experienced His life amongst them.

For those who are discovering Jesus anew today there is a need for sound teaching and guidance, as to how to proceed; how to grow, how to become mature adults in the new life; in the kingdom that He has made available for us.

This book sets out to address that need in part.

Peter's words at Pentecost:

"So let everyone in Israel know for certain that God has made this Jesus, whom you crucified, to be both Lord and Messiah!"

Peter's words pierced their hearts, and they said to him and to the other apostles, "Brothers, what should we do?"

Peter replied, "Each of you must repent of your sins and turn to God, and be baptised in the name of Jesus Christ for the forgiveness of your sins.

Then you will receive the gift of the Holy Spirit.

This promise is to you, to your children, and to those far away—all who have been called by the Lord our God."
The Acts of the Apostles 2:38-39.

Our Entrance into God's Kingdom of Life:

In many ways Peter's guidance, that we can find in chapter two of The Acts of the Apostles, covers all that we need to know and to proceed with in our new life with Jesus.

Whilst Jesus was still with His disciples on earth He promised that after He had returned to His Father He would send another counsellor. Some translations refer to Holy Spirit as a comforter or advocate. The Greek word used in scripture is, *'paraclete'*, and can be translated as an encourager as well.

"But I will send you the Advocate —the Spirit of truth.
He will come to you from the Father and will testify all about me.'
John 15:26.

Jesus described Holy Spirit as the Spirit of Truth.

Jesus also referred to Himself as being Truth on occasions.

'Jesus told him, "I am the way, the truth, and the life. No one can come to the Father except through me. '
John 14:6.

The disciples were very sad to experience Jesus leaving and did not know what would occur as a consequence

of all that He had done, but as they were together on the day of Pentecost they had the amazing experience of Holy Spirit descending upon each one of them like flames of fire.
They heard a sound like a mighty storm and wind.

All of the disciples experienced the same thing.

They were filled with the Holy Spirit and began speaking in other languages.

The people who heard them came running and were amazed to find that they could understand each one speaking in their own language.

The crowd believed them to be drunk but Peter assured them that they were not as it was still very early in the morning.
The Acts of the Apostles 2:1-36.

Having explained all that Jesus achieved during His life Peter went on to tell the crowd what they must do:

These are very briefly his words of guidance:

1. Repent from our past lives.
2. Turn to God - Believe in Jesus - understand and trust in what He has achieved on our behalf.
3. Be baptised into the name of Jesus.
4. Receive the gift of His Spirit.

We will be looking into these four headlines in more detail but the truth is that when we have realised where we are now and consider what Jesus has done for us and how we have ignored and even rebelled against God, we will want to change; to turn around and head in a different direction.

We will want to leave behind the life that we have lived previously, to apologise for our past life with a desire for a life lived with Jesus: a life of righteousness.

Having then entered God's kingdom, through faith in what Jesus achieved on our behalf, being baptised into the all powerful and overwhelming name of Jesus and receiving the gift of His Spirit, we have all that we need for the new, full and overcoming life that is to be experienced in His kingdom.

We will now discover why that is so.

What do those four directions mean for us in detail?

Two opposing kingdoms:

In order to get an understanding of what Peter's words meant; to realise what Jesus has achieved during His time on earth, we need to first place ourselves in the shoes of those living at that time and to understand the situation they were in prior to Jesus's ministry here.

The overriding situation for those who lived prior to the life of Jesus can be explained simply, and that is one of utter hopelessness.

To get a better picture we need to return to the beginning of time.

Father had created a world in which man and woman were living in oneness with Him.

We have outlined the history of the fall of man elsewhere and so a brief catch up here will suffice for our understanding.

Mankind's rebellion towards God, sin, has created a division between man and the God who loves us.

There was no way for man to become one with God again as God is Holy and man is sinful.

The best that we could hope for, and what those who knew God were looking for, was some sort of redeemer;

a Messiah, who God had promised to send one day, to repair the break in our unity with Him.

Until that time the only hope that we had was to adhere to a set of rules that God had given to Moses, to keep ourselves ritually clean through the sacrifice of animals and to hope that after our death our souls would one day be restored by the Messiah who was promised.

At the time of Jesus, the religious priests and leaders of the Jewish nation had so corrupted the laws of Moses and added hundreds of sub clauses and variations to these laws that it had become virtually impossible to understand the rules and much less to keep them all.

The laws had been used to create divisions between the wealthy and the poor and even the leading rabbi's continually argued as to how to interpret what were once simple guidelines that God had given.

The priests had originally been appointed to guide the tribes of Israel, to teach them the things of God, to act as caretakers to keep the nation holy; a nation that represented God on earth but their role had been replaced by hypocrisy and a greed for power.

Jesus called them *'whitewashed tombs, which look clean on the outside but inside were full of decay and dead bones'. Matthew 23:27.*

For the population of Israel there was little hope but to do the best that they could during life and then to die hoping that their ritual acts of sacrifice, and having a heart that was turned to God, would bring an eventual redemption.

There were few who understood that those ritual acts were only an external picture of what was in our heart.

Our works, or 'sacrifices' can never please God who looks at our hearts to see if our desires are towards Him or whether we are simply attempting to work our way into a blessing.

Sacrifices alone could never bridge the gap that had occurred between God and man, but a pure heart such as one that King David, other prophets and men of God who desired to please God had, drew Him to them.

Whilst God had given the laws and sacrifices as a manner in which the people could recognise sin and to become pure again on a temporary basis, God looks for relationships and not sacrifices.

In truth God saw through the hearts of those who brought sacrifices with an unclean heart and told them:

*I am sick of your burnt offerings of rams
and the fat of fattened cattle.
I get no pleasure from the blood
of bulls and lambs and goats.*

When you come to worship me, who asked you to parade through my courts with all your ceremony?
Stop bringing me your meaningless gifts;
the incense of your offerings disgusts me!
Isaiah 1:11-13.

On the other hand King David knew, for sure, that his soul would not be left in the grave.
He could confidently write thus:

For you will not leave my soul among the dead or allow your holy one to rot in the grave.
Psalms 16:10

Jesus came at a time when there was a hunger in the Jewish nation for change.

Many thousands flocked to hear the news of the kingdom and to witness the power of Holy Spirit; the authority of God, as Jesus cast out demons, healed the sick, raised the dead and taught them of the things of the kingdom that He had come to establish on earth.

The news of God's kingdom was in truth, very good news indeed for those who had been looking for Jesus' coming.

Jesus was the son of God.
He was the answer to many thousands of years of waiting for a Messiah; a redeemer.

Jesus was the one who could restore mankind into unity with God.

He was the only one who could do that as He was the only pure and sinless person.

Israel had, for thousands of years been taught from the laws of Moses that only a pure and unblemished lamb could suffice as a sacrifice for their sin.

Jesus was that Holy, pure and unblemished lamb that God had supplied from Himself.

He was the one time perfect sacrifice.

The life of Jesus was one that was built upon and lived out in love and obedience for Father and for us.

Jesus was crucified and after three days He was raised from the dead.
Because He had no sin, death had no claim on Him, He overcame the power that death had up to that time.

To explain in different words, He had overcome death.
And not only death but all the sin of rebellion that had entered into the world since the fall of man.

Because of what Jesus achieved, nothing of evil that once had power to cause harm, has any power over us any longer unless we allow it.

Jesus was the perfect sacrifice and He achieved a perfect and all encompassing victory on our behalf.

He achieved all of that for us if we have faith in Him; if we trust in Him.

We can believe that His sacrifice is sufficient to restore us to God.

Our faith in the achievement of Jesus is the beginning of our entry into His kingdom.

As a consequence of what Jesus achieved we are able to leave the kingdom of death that we are all born into and to enter His kingdom of life.

We do not need to wait, as David and others did, for the Messiah to come for our restoration; that one day our souls might be raised from the grave.

Jesus has fulfilled that role entirely on our behalf. We are able to be freed from the law that previously had control over us; the law of sin and death, immediately, today.

This is the good news that Peter preached about at Pentecost.
It is the reason that Jesus came to earth.

Paul wrote to the Roman christians about this good news:

This Good News tells us how God makes us right in his sight.
This is accomplished from start to finish by faith.
As the Scriptures say, "It is through faith that a righteous person has life."
Romans 1:17.

To Repent:

Peter's first word of advice to the crowds listening, was to repent.

What do these words mean?

In truth the phrase 'to repent' is a slight distortion of the words that Peter used.

Peter used the Greek word, *'metanoia'*, which means to have a change of mind.

Some describe his words as a desire to turn around and travel in a different direction or to rethink the way we live.

Our English word, repent, comes from a latin translation of the Greek, which isn't a good translation.

It also includes the implication of doing penance and so we get the word 're-penance' or repentance.

Doing penance is not what Peter was advising at all.

There are some who suggest that doing penance is a good thing, in contrast to what scripture teaches us.

Jesus has taken away our sin once and for all.
His sacrifice is sufficient, there is no requirement for penance in any way.

There can never be any penance that we could carry out that is greater than the loving sacrifice that Jesus made on our behalf and His sacrifice covers all of our sin; all of our rebellion, for all time.

Peter was describing a realisation that we need a restoration to God.

We live in rebellion to Him. That rebellion is called sin as it describes a life lived outside of: without consideration of God.

When we realise that truth, we can acknowledge our fault and apologise.
We can say that we are sorry and we want to be restored to Him.

Peter's word, *'metanoia'*, describes a desire to turn around, to become different; to walk through life in a different way.

There is a reason why Peter placed repentance at the foremost of the actions that we must take.

The importance of our repentance can not be overemphasised.

If there is no conviction of sin within us and therefore no repentance, we will have no foundation to build upon.

The deeper our repentance: our sorrow upon the realisation of our situation, and our desire to please God instead, the greater will be our effectiveness in our new life.

Many difficulties: hurdles, and reasons for our failures occur as a consequence of our not first establishing a deep foundation in our entry to the kingdom.

Some of those difficulties arise from a misunderstanding of baptism, but the lack of sincere repentance also plays a big part.

We will soon be discovering how to live in righteousness and this is the direction that we now wish to travel in as a response to what Jesus has achieved for us.

We will struggle with these battles unless good foundations are in place.

Previously we had no desire or ability to walk in a different way. We lived in independence from God.

Sin was the ruling factor in our lives but as a consequence of what Jesus has achieved we will now have the power to overcome those desires and those powerful urges to sin.

Before we were powerless, we inevitably did wrong in many ways:

Our selfishness propelled us to please ourselves first. Our greed propelled us to have a desire for money or control over others.

Our jealousy caused us to say unpleasant things, deceit caused us to have secrets, our fears and addictions kept us in chains of isolation and restriction.

But when we enter God's kingdom those overpowering urges fall away and we become free from them.

We are then free to serve Jesus, in contrast to leading a life that will be filled with self will, one that is leading inevitably to end in death.

Peter's words, 'repent', then are very apt.
Realising what Jesus has achieved we can be sorry for the way we have lived our lives and have a desire to turn around.

Repentance is the first foundation stone in our new life.

Restoration can only come after repentance. We cannot have one without the other.

Unless we are truly sorry, realising what we have done in our rebellion towards God: who we are and of our realisation of our need for a saviour, we will not be able to establish any further foundations.

A conviction of our own sin is the first indication that we are being offered a solution to our state.

We first need to respond to the conviction in humble acceptance and apology. We need to say sorry and to have a desire to change.

We can have that desire, but in truth, there is little we can do about changing ourselves without God's hand in our lives.

This is why we need to have faith in Jesus, to be baptised in His name and to have God's Spirit become one with us.

Then we will begin to become changed to being like Him.

We will move on to this need next.

To Believe in Jesus:

Peter's words given to the crowds in response to their question: what must we do? are, to 'turn to God'.

These words of guidance are encompassed within the phrase to 'repent'.

We might imagine the awe and wonder, perhaps mingled with shame and humility at the question from the crowd.

What must we do?
What can we do?

How can we respond to what we have done to Jesus, the Messiah, how do we respond to the realisation we now have, of sin in our lives? but also, how do we respond to His love towards us?

And how do we respond to the implications of His sacrifice for us?

A door has opened! An opportunity has been given!
A unique invitation is offered to us!

Peter's crowd were standing at the very centre of history.
This was an event, an occasion, a period that had never occurred before.

What Jesus had achieved had changed everything.
The world had been turned upside down.

They were standing at the dawn of a new era: a new beginning.

They were the first of a new creation.
They asked, 'what must we do'?

How do we respond?
Tell us Peter.

Peter's response was; 'turn to God'.

God has provided the answer to that question.
The answer is Jesus.

The crowd understood that something awesome was occurring and had occurred.

They had crucified the son of God but He had risen from the dead, overpowering the law of sin and death.

Jesus had returned to His Father and sent His Spirit which had fallen on His followers.

The crowd understood the prophecies that had given notice of these things happening.

The prophet Joel spoke over four hundred years earlier about these things that were happening in front of their eyes.

"Then, after doing all those things,
I will pour out my Spirit upon all people.
Your sons and daughters will prophesy.
Your old men will dream dreams,
and your young men will see visions.
In those days I will pour out my Spirit
even on servants—men and women alike.
Joel 2:28-29.

These people were Jews and had been taught these things and so realised that what Peter was telling them was true.

They now understood that the answer is Jesus.

Jesus has always been God's master plan. He has always been the answer, from the foundation of the earth.

The crowd knew about God, they had faith in God but Jesus was an added dimension.

Jesus is Life. He is the Way and the Truth.
Those are not only names for Jesus, but the names are who He is.
Where there is truth, there is Jesus.
Where there is a way; guidance, there is Jesus.

Where there is true life, there is Jesus.

In Peter's words, 'turn to God', lies all that we need to know.
God has provided the answer in Jesus.

Trust Him - He brings security - He brings Life - He brings all that we need.
He brings forgiveness - salvation - promise, hope.
All things flow from our relationship, our trust in Him.

In the question from the crowd listening to Peter were the implications of, how can we be forgiven for what we have done?

Forgiveness lies in Jesus.

We can trust that He will forgive us. That was why He came and suffered.
He had each one of us on His mind at that time.

The joy of knowing our forgiveness was what spurred Him on; the joy of knowing that we can become one with Him.

He asked Father if there was another way for that aim to be achieved, but there wasn't and so He went through with the ordeal so that we could receive forgiveness and to become one with us.

That has always been the Father's promise to us.

Jesus constantly prayed towards that end because that is His Fathers desire as well:

*"I am praying not only for these disciples but also for all who will ever believe in me through their message.
I pray that they will all be one, just as you and I are one—as you are in me, Father, and I am in you.
And may they be in us so that the world will believe you sent me.
John 17:20-21.*

Jesus prayed not only for His followers to be one with each other but that each one of us would be one with the Godhead as well: a complete and entire restoration.

The crowd followed Peter's advice and turned to God - He had the answer, and that day three thousand people entered the kingdom through the door, who is Jesus.

A short time later Peter and John were hauled before the courts because they had healed a crippled man.

They were asked by whose name they had healed the man.
Peter told them that his authority came from Jesus who they had crucified.
At that time Peter stood before the religious leaders and advised them thus:

There is salvation in no one else! God has given no other name under heaven by which we must be saved." Acts 4:12.

By now there were five thousand people who were following Jesus.

Be Baptised:

The act of baptising in water originates from the ritual washing that was carried out by the Levitical priests during the temple period.

Although simple washing in water had no ability to wash away the sins of the priests, it was carried out by way of a symbolic gesture which emphasised the reality that they were impure and that there was a need to become symbolically pure or clean before entering into the presence of God.

Other religions today carry out similar gestures when entering into prayer which also have no physical ability to make a person sinless but are gestures which recognise a sinful state.

John who was called John the baptiser, baptised those who came to him recognising the need to repent from a life apart from God.

This symbolised a washing of sin from the body and indicated a desire to serve God.

John's baptism of repentance, whilst serving as a temporary reminder of a change of heart, and desire to serve God, could not physically change a person's thought processes or the manner in which a person might respond to the temptation to sin.

John's baptism was a public display indicating a desire for God but had no lasting effect on a person's life other than a self determination to please God.

It lacked any tangible power that might enable a person to change.

John spoke of one who was coming after Him who would baptise with power.

*"I baptise with water those who repent of their sins and turn to God. But someone is coming soon who is greater than I am—so much greater that I'm not worthy even to be his slave and carry his sandals.
He will baptise you with the Holy Spirit and with fire".*
Matthew 3:11.

It is only through baptism into God's Spirit that we can be endued with power to bring about change: power to overcome the works of the enemy that seek to harm us and the power to perform miracles as Jesus did, in order to display the establishment of God's kingdom.

Without baptism, we do not receive the power of God's Spirit and we are therefore unable to carry out the works that we have been chosen to do.

We remain much as we were before we came to Jesus and of little use within the kingdom, unable to defend ourselves against the onslaughts of the enemy.

We remain immature and will be easily picked off and left for dead spiritually.

The fire that John spoke about refers to the cleansing fire that comes from God which is a purifier.

As gold is purified in a fire, removing the impurities, so are we passed through a fire; trials and testing times, that will remove impure thoughts that lead to rebellious deeds. We are purified into living righteously.

It is only through baptism into the name of Jesus that we receive power and are enabled to be brought to a full spiritual maturity leading to righteousness.

Being righteous simply means living rightly with God.

In order to understand this a little better we will look at what happened when Jesus asked John to baptise Him.

Jesus came to John the baptiser and asked to be baptised.
John's response was that Jesus was sinless, He had no need of repentance, He had no need to be baptised.

Jesus knew better, Jesus's desire to be baptised didn't come from a need to repent, as ours might be, but from a desire to please His Father; a desire to be obedient in everything.

But John tried to talk him out of it. *"I am the one who needs to be baptised by you,"* he said, *"so why are you coming to me?"*
But Jesus said, *"It should be done, for we must carry out all that God requires."*
So John agreed to baptise him.
Matthew 3:14-15.

Jesus wanted to carry out 'all that was required'.

Other bible versions translate Jesus' words as, *"permit it now, in order to fulfil all righteousness"*.

It is our new ability to be able to both hear Father and to please Him that is creating a righteousness within us.

Through baptism we are able to hear His voice in our spiritual ear, we are able to obey His instruction and teaching, we can comprehend His discipline and guidance through difficult times and we can live in His presence.

It was when Jesus was baptised that God spoke and said, *"this is my beloved Son in whom I am well pleased and delighted"!*

Father delights in our obedience.

Holy Spirit then descended upon Jesus.

Had Jesus listened to John and not been baptised by Him He would not have received Holy Spirit, who brought Him the power that enabled Him to carry out His ministry on earth.

It was after His baptism that Jesus experienced the temptations of satan in the desert and was able to overcome him there.

Those who knew Jesus before His baptism remarked on the change that had occurred when they met Him afterwards.

'He returned to Nazareth, his hometown. When he taught there in the synagogue, everyone was amazed and said, "Where does he get this wisdom and the power to do miracles?" '
Then they said, "He's just the carpenter's son, and we know Mary, his mother, and his brothers—James, Joseph, Simon, and Judas.
All his sisters live right here among us. Where did he learn all these things?"
Matthew 13:54-56.

Baptism in faith brings about change.

There are many today who deny the need for baptism. Jesus knew better.

It is only through baptism that we are affirmed by Father.

It is only through baptism that we receive authority to carry out the works of Father.

Our obedience to Father produces righteousness that produces further opportunities to be obedient through additional opportunities to carry out His will.

If we fail in the first trial, in being obedient through baptism, we will inevitably fail through other opportunities should they be forthcoming.

Unless we are obedient in being baptised there will be no authority from Father in our lives, despite our eagerness, or natural charisma.

Whilst John's Baptism was useful in providing a focus for the need for repentance, it is only baptism into the name of Jesus that provides power to bring about change, a change in ourselves and also power to overcome the works of the enemy who seeks to destroy.

The reason that Jesus' name can produce real change is a factor that is called faith.

It is our faith in what Jesus has achieved on our behalf that will bring us into salvation: redemption.

We believe what Jesus has promised.

Faith is able to produce something that did not previously exist.

Faith is the formula that is creative - it makes real that which has been promised.

We can be given many promises by God, but until we activate those promises by our faith they will not become a reality for us, without faith they will remain only promises; only words.

The principle is the same with baptism as it is with all of God's promises, as it is with all that Jesus achieved on our behalf.
Faith is the ingredient that produces activity - reality.

We must activate our faith in order to receive His life.

If we have been promised healing we must activate our faith in order to bring that healing about.

God's promises are always secure but they are dependent upon our response, our faith in Him, in believing that what He has promised He will carry out.

Simply being baptised in water will not produce anything but perhaps a bodily cleansing.

It is through faith that we are baptised into His name, into all that He is and that we receive the same power that raised Jesus from the dead.

It was Paul when writing to the Roman christians who explained:

The Spirit of God, who raised Jesus from the dead, lives in you. And just as God raised Christ Jesus from the dead, he will give life to your mortal bodies by this same Spirit living within you.
Romans 8:11.

The truth is that we can only gain a spiritual position which Jesus has first claimed for Himself.
And He gained every position so that we can follow Him into it.

Therefore, because He was baptised to fulfil all righteousness, to be recognised as the Son of God and to be released under the authority of His Father, we must be baptised to gain what He has claimed for us.

We have talked about being baptised into the name of Jesus.

There are some who baptise in the name of the Father or the Son or Holy Spirit, often all three names are invoked, and so why baptise in the name of Jesus?

In the following verse Jesus is telling the disciples that they are to baptise others with the authority of the Father, the Son and Holy Spirit.

Therefore, go and make disciples of all the nations, baptising them in the name of the Father and the Son and the Holy Spirit. '

Matthew 28:19.

This is about the authority that we have to baptise others, we are acting in God's name, we have His authority to baptise, but we baptise them into the name of Jesus.

Paul had authority from God to baptise as we do, but he baptised into the name of Jesus:
'As soon as they heard this, they were baptised into the name of the Lord Jesus.'
Acts of the Apostles 19:5

Luke also wrote of new converts being baptised into the name of Jesus:
Acts 8:12,16-17 (by Philip); 10:48. (by Peter) Acts 19:5. (by Paul)

Why into the name of Jesus?

The word 'into', which is the correct translation from the Greek, rather than, 'in', implies movement.

We are being transformed from one position into another: from death into life, from being outside of God's kingdom to being inside.

The name Jesus means "Saviour", and Jesus saves whenever we have faith for Him to act.

Jesus has many names, each one carrying power for us to experience: He is Lord of every situation.
He is the Healer, the Provider, and many others.

When we enter His name, we gain everything within Him, if we have revelation and faith.

Jesus is the door. Jesus is the way. Jesus is the truth. Jesus is life. Jesus gives us access to His Kingdom. *John 14:6.*

Faith in the sacrifice of Jesus on the cross gives us salvation from rejection by God.
We receive all that Jesus achieved on the cross when we are baptised.
Baptism is the door into salvation from sin and a wasted life.

In baptism God is performing a spiritual transformation: we are being transformed from death into life.

In baptism we make an exchange. We give Satan our old nature and we receive God's nature.

Our old nature belongs to Satan.
Therefore, we give it to him.
We have no need for it any longer because we receive Holy Spirit, and the fruit of Holy Spirit can begin to create our new nature.

Without baptism, our old nature continues to have a legal power over us.
But we die to that power when we break covenant with darkness.

That is why people are healed, set free from demons, and experience the power of God in many ways when they form a new covenant with God in baptism.

If we are still living in a covenant with Satan, we are restricted in the works we can do with God.
God can still use us, but we are not legally His servant.

When we are baptised, we become part of the world-wide Body of Christ. We are baptised into the Body of Christ, fully immersed and not on the sidelines.

We immediately become a functioning part of the Body because we have become alive in Holy Spirit.

We can function because it is Holy Spirit wisdom and gifts which we now have.
We have died to the foolish ideas of our old life and have the revelation of God to share - we have become one with Him.

This is only valid when we have a revelation of the death and life of baptism.

Paul came across some believers who had not been baptised into the name of Jesus on his way to Ephesus one day, they had only received John's baptism of repentance. They were not aware of Holy Spirit.

Paul immediately recognised by their lives, their speech, by the lack of the presence of God, that they did not know God.

While Apollos was in Corinth, Paul travelled through the interior regions until he reached Ephesus, on the coast, where he found several believers.
"Did you receive the Holy Spirit when you believed?" he asked them.
"No," they replied, "we haven't even heard that there is a Holy Spirit."
"Then what baptism did you experience?" he asked.
And they replied, "The baptism of John."

Paul said, "John's baptism called for repentance from sin.
But John himself told the people to believe in the one who would come later, meaning Jesus."

As soon as they heard this, they were baptised in the name of the Lord Jesus.
Then when Paul laid his hands on them, the Holy Spirit came on them, and they spoke in other tongues and prophesied.
There were about twelve men in all.
Acts 19:1-7.

If we do not die to the old nature, we continue to live with foolish ideas and a fallen mind.

But if we live in the new nature of Spirit God, we have His wisdom to share.

That is why the Ephesian disciples who Paul baptised, immediately began to prophesy after their baptism.

They were disciples before their baptism.
But they only received Holy Spirit by being baptised.

In baptism we enter into a covenant with God.

It is not a covenant that is dependent upon us but it is a covenant that He has prepared for us. It is a gift, given freely from him and is as a consequence of what Jesus has achieved for us.

Then you will receive the Gift of Holy Spirit:

Peter then advised the crowds, who were eager to discover what they might do, that they would receive the gift of Holy Spirit.

This promise was not a flimsy suggestion of something that might happen, but a secure promise of something that he knew was a sure thing.

When we respond to God He will always deliver on His promise. He can do no other.

Simply saying a prayer in response to an evangelist or putting our hand in the air, to express our realisation of sin, will never bring a response from God, let alone transform us or the world around us.

We need to be wholehearted in our response to God. We must convert our understanding, our revelation, into action: we must respond in obedience.

Then we will receive the gift of Holy Spirit who will impart to us the power that enables us to live in the kingdom we have inherited.

Holy Spirit is the third person of God.
Holy Spirit is the movement, the activity, the power, of God.

It is Holy Spirit who will abide with us for all time when we become one with God.

Without Holy Spirit we have nothing of God with us and are simply living a ritualistic life, going through religious motions which can never produce life.

Without Holy Spirit we will inevitably reproduce others who continue with the same lifeless activities: those who do not know God for themselves and have no life within them.

Holy Spirit produces life. He is creative.

It is Holy Spirit who has the ability to produce change in us, through our obedience to His promptings and by changing our thought patterns.

Holy Spirit will train us into righteousness.

There are those who might choose to reject Holy Spirit: to attempt to continue serving God through their own abilities. There are many who do.

They survive by working hard, carrying out good works.

Some have natural charisma and can convince many through their words and grand preaching, but in truth unless and until God gives us authorisation, unless we are serving him, being guided by Holy Spirit, our works will come to nothing and we will remain outside of God's kingdom.

In the end Jesus will deny us having never known Him in truth.

Paul spoke of such people in his letter to Timothy:
They will act religious, but they will reject the power that could make them godly.
Stay away from people like that!
2 Timothy 3:5.

There was one person who Jesus promised would be with Him when He came back to claim His kingdom who was not baptised and did not receive Holy Spirit.

The thief, who died with Jesus on the cross had no time for baptism and did not need to receive the power of Holy Spirit in order to be able to overcome during his life as he died very shortly after acknowledging Jesus.

A death bed conversion is not advisable and may be construed as being false. Only God knows our heart.

We may wonder, when we know the truth of Jesus, why would we wait?

However, it is not possible for us to live in God's kingdom without the gift of Holy Spirit in our lives.

The power that we are given is varied and limitless.

Jesus said that despite doing many miraculous acts, we would carry out many more and greater works:
"I tell you the truth, anyone who believes in me will do the same works I have done, and even greater works, because I am going to be with the Father. '
John 14:12.

Holy Spirit is the factor that will enable us to carry out those works.

Holy Spirit is the one who will bring revelation to us, enabling change and freedom in our own lives.

We cannot overcome the works of the enemy unless we have authority from Father and the gift of Holy Spirit.

Peter continued preaching to the crowd saying:

This promise is to you, to your children, and to those far away—all who have been called by the Lord our God."

Then Peter continued preaching for a long time, strongly urging all his listeners, "Save yourselves from this crooked generation!"
The Acts of the Apostles 2:39-40.

The promise of God is for you and for me and for our children.

The promise is dependent upon our response.

Had Jesus responded differently to the events in His life, to the challenges He faced, to John, who suggested He didn't need to be baptised, to the leaders and priests who wanted Him crucified and yet found no evidence to carry out their threats and to all of the various types of opposition that He faced throughout His life on a daily basis, there would be no promise for us.

How will we respond?

There is no other way for us to be saved, both for eternity and for each one of our daily lives.

We are living in God's kingdom.

We began our book by stating that, in many ways Peter's words of advice are all that we need to continue in our walk with God.

We have laid a good foundation that is based upon obedience in hearing Fathers instructions.

That obedience is carried out by using our faith in what we know to be true.

The followers of Jesus had no other guidance than that of the Hebrew scriptures and the word of God in their ear.

Jesus had trained the disciples to be able to hear Father.

Holy Spirit spoke to them and recalled to them the words of Jesus as well as bringing them daily revelation and realisation of all that Father wanted them to know.

We can now read of their lives and the letters of guidance and teaching that they wrote to others that will also help us in our new life.

Their lives were guided by faith in what they knew to be true and by Holy Spirit who is the Spirit of Truth.

We also need no other guidance than the way in which they were equipped by Jesus.

Jesus had told His disciples that when Holy Spirit came He would show them the truth:

'When the Spirit of truth comes, he will guide you into all truth. He will not speak on his own but will tell you what he has heard. He will tell you about the future'.
John 16:13.

In truth, Holy Spirit is the only leader and teacher that we need.
This is something that Jesus emphasised to His disciples:

"Don't let anyone call you 'Rabbi,' for you have only one teacher, and all of you are equal as brothers and sisters. And don't address anyone here on earth as 'Father,' for only God in heaven is your Father.
And don't let anyone call you 'Teacher,' for you have only one teacher, the Messiah.
Matthew 23:8-10.

We have not had the benefit of Jesus' personal teaching but included within those words of Jesus is the reminder and instruction that we are baptised into a family; we are true brothers and sisters.

We are all equal and we are one family of God.

Each one of us has the same Spirit and we are all able to hear Father individually in order to encourage and to teach each other according to what Father is saying to us at any time.

We do not need to appoint a third party, an intermediary, to hear from God on our behalf.

To create a hierarchy of special ministers or leaders is to go against all that Jesus taught.

We are responsible for each other, we serve each other and there is no single ministry that becomes responsible for the whole family except Jesus, who is the head.

The position that some assume as 'leaders' or 'pastors' within the church community today is far removed from the example that Jesus gave.

I have given this subject more time in other places but I will mention it briefly here.

When we read of leaders within the community of God in the letters within the bible we find that these are not appointed to minister 'over' the body but are equal with and a part of, not supported or financed by the body but serving the body.

The picture of one who leads in scripture is that of a mentor, an elder, or one who is more spiritually mature who is able to come alongside others and teach or minister in some other way according to their gifting.

Each one of the more spiritually mature could lead in a given situation dependent upon gifting.

There is no independent or single, one man ministry or team of ministers within God's 'ekklesia'.

We are all of one mind, and each one of us is able to hear from Father.
As we are all baptised into Jesus, we all have the same Spirit who speaks to each one of us for the benefit of us all.

The appointment of ministers in that way inevitably excludes others from participating in the body of Jesus.

The manner in which the churches today are governed is more in line with the old temple system that Jesus came to replace.

The foundation of the family of God is one that is built upon love.

We will learn how that love for each other is manifested as we grow towards maturity.

Whilst we are young spiritually we will want to check the things that we say and do as to whether our motivations are of love for another or whether they come from a desire to serve ourselves.

God is love and therefore if we are born of Him His love will become one with us also.

Our love for others within the family of God will produce life.

We will learn to encourage, to care, to share our sufferings and our joys.

Holy Spirit will enable us to minister to each other, and to those who do not yet know Jesus, by using the spiritual gifts that He gives to us.

These may be by prophesying in words of encouragement, words of knowledge and wisdom, in teaching and in training.

We may have gifts of hospitality in entertaining others in our homes or by way of supporting those in need.

We will learn kindness, peace and a joy that those in the world cannot experience.

Our security will become based on all that Jesus provides rather than ourselves.

Some of us may have a gift of healing and be able to carry out miraculous acts.

There is no limit to the gifts that Holy Spirit will supply for our needs.

In Paul's letters he emphasises the need to learn how to love and to be able to exercise all that we do in a spirit of love.

God is love and so as we become one with Him we will surely take on His nature also.

This is how the world will recognise those who belong to Him.

Life in the Kingdom:

When Peter had finished speaking, Luke, in his account of the events, had given us a picture of the manner in which the new followers lived.

Very briefly, we read that they had everything in common and met daily, eating together, to receive teaching and their numbers grew daily.
Acts of the Apostles 2:42-47.

Our own personal, spiritual growth and maturity will come about as a response to our sharing our lives with others.

We read earlier that after John and Peter were taken to court there were five thousand followers.

I am pretty sure five thousand souls would not have met together in a person's home at the same time.

But the disciples taught them and as they grew in spiritual strength and maturity they taught each other.

The home was the natural place for them to meet together and to learn from each other.

Such was their bond that they sold what they had in order to bring support to those in need.

There was unity and love between them all.

Many miraculous acts were carried out and they were all in deep awe and wonder.

There would have been plenty to talk about and to enjoy together when they met.

When the disciples were writing letters some sixty to ninety years later the followers of Jesus were still meeting in each other's homes.

The home is the natural place for christians to meet up and to share the life of Jesus.

In the home we are able to focus on Jesus rather than anything or anyone else.

The home is where we naturally exhibit a loving nature or otherwise, it is where we interact with our family and friends.
We are able to offer hospitality there and lodging if anyone is in need.

It is in the home, our workplace and in our social gatherings that who we are is displayed.

It is in those arenas that the world will see whether Jesus lives among us, or not.

It wasn't until some three hundred years later that the Emperor Constantine initiated a counterfeit religion, appointing priests in buildings that resembled temples, and forbad the meeting of christians in homes, that buildings became the only place to go.

Despite Constantine's efforts, groups of christians still met together, secretly, risking their lives in order to be able to serve Jesus intimately.

The early christians knew from experience that they were able to minister to each other and to God better within small groups.

Jesus had told them that where two or three were gathered together He was there with them.

"I also tell you this: If two of you agree here on earth concerning anything you ask, my Father in heaven will do it for you.

For where two or three gather together as my followers, I am there among them."
Matthew 18:19-20.

Small numbers of people are far closer in their relationships.
Better relationships can be forged intimately within a small group setting.

Go does not care for large numbers but He is interested in intimate relationships.

54

It is good for large numbers to be born again but fellowship needs intimacy in order to flourish and for us to grow into maturity..

God's kingdom is not dependent upon numbers but the flesh and bones of His kingdom is built on relationships; the closer they are, the stronger the kingdom becomes.

The kingdom grew as a consequence of the intimacy: the love that was shared amongst these small groupings.

During the first century as the kingdom was expanding rapidly, there may have been thousands of followers within a city, such as there were in Rome or Ephesus.

Each small group met in homes but they were not exclusive to each other.

Letters would be passed around the town, people would move from group to group, teaching and ministering.

There would be plenty of coming and going between groups, sharing the life of Jesus, sharing news, sharing miracles, sharing needs.

Today, church leaders depend upon a congregation to support them financially. This is not the way in which Jesus taught His followers.

They refer to themselves as shepherds but where do we find that sheep support the shepherd? The idea is contrary to nature as well as to the teaching of Jesus.

We read earlier where Jesus taught us not to have hierarchies but to be equal as brothers and sisters; there is only one teacher and He is God.

Paul and other writers were very scathing of the way false teachers undermined the truth whilst asking for money for their keep.

It is because leaders today need a large congregation to support them that they incorrectly use the words of scripture.
The writer of the letter to the Hebrews wrote thus:

And let us not neglect our meeting together, as some people do, but encourage one another, especially now that the day of his return is drawing near.
Hebrews 10:25.

The writer is encouraging people to meet together to share the life of Jesus but he is not encouraging them to attend a church building. There were no church buildings and no church.

The concept of church as we know it today was not known and is not mentioned anywhere in scripture.

On the contrary, many of the letters that are written by the Apostles warn against much of the false teaching that is entertained in today's church systems.

The body of people that Jesus taught about, who would become His followers, and those who His disciples baptised into His kingdom are given the Greek title of *'the ekklesia'*.

The word describes a group of people who are taken out of a community and given a specific purpose such as a jury, or a council might.

If we have come into God's kingdom we are taken out from the world and given the specific purpose of serving God, in the establishment of His kingdom on earth.

We are *'the ekklesia'* of God.

The kingdom that we now live in is built upon relationships. The closer those relationships are, the stronger we will be.

We may find that it is necessary at times to meet within a building that is not a home but we should be aware that our foremost aim is to build relationships and not dogma or doctrine.

Jesus prayed that we would live in unity with each other, united in thought and deed in line with Fathers ambitions for us: in order to reflect Jesus to the dying world around us.

The kingdom is built upon love exhibited by lives lived with each other.

It is only when the world can see the life of the kingdom that they will comprehend the good news.

Christians:

It was at Antioch that the followers of Jesus were first called christians.

During the period of circa 30 - 36 A.D. there had been a persecution of the followers of Jesus and Stephen had been stoned to death.

Some followers who had dispersed to Cyprus and Cyrene decided to begin speaking in Antioch and many Gentiles (people who were not Jews) received Jesus as Lord there.

The disciples, who were still in Jerusalem, sent a man named Barnabus to find out what was happening.

Barnabus saw that many people were being brought into the kingdom and so he sent for Saul from Tarsus, who was later named Paul.

When he found him, he brought him back to Antioch. Both of them stayed there with the ekklesia for a full year, teaching large crowds of people.
(It was at Antioch that the believers were first called Christians.)
The Acts of the Apostles 11:26.

This was one of the first occasions that Gentiles had turned to the Lord and it is interesting to see that they behaved so much like Christ that people began calling them 'Christ-ones' or christians as the expression has now become.

When we spend time with Jesus, we too will begin to reflect Jesus to the world: His character will begin to become one with us.

We will do the works that Jesus began because our thoughts will be focussed on Him rather than ourselves.

To live in the likeness of Jesus is not simply a pie in the sky idea but this is the reality of living as one with each other and with Him.

The prophet Isaiah gave us these words from the Lord:

"My thoughts are nothing like your thoughts," says the Lord.
"And my ways are far beyond anything you could imagine.
For just as the heavens are higher than the earth,
so my ways are higher than your ways and my thoughts higher than your thoughts.
Isaiah 55:8-9.

But now that we have God's Spirit living amongst us God's thoughts do become our thoughts and as we grow in maturity that becomes ever more the truth.

We are unable to say at the present time that we live in unity with each other, whilst there are many denominations and different groupings within close proximity who do not fellowship together, although we may have close relationships with some.

We must strive to break the barriers that we have created in order to become one, with Jesus as our focus.

At present our focus is on building walls, stronger power bases and larger congregations to serve our own purposes.

Our visions are introverted, focussing on what we are able to do in our strengths but that is not the way of the kingdom.

It is only through our unity; our oneness, that the enemy will be defeated and removed from the places that are still under his control.

We reflect Jesus to the world when we focus on Him and on His kingdom.

While we focus on building our own kingdom, reinforcing our doctrines and rituals, within our own fortresses the world will only see division and weakness.

All that is opposed to God's kingdom will eventually be pulled down.

We would do well to get in line with God's plan before we too are brought low.

But as we live in the light of His Truth we will continue to build His kingdom: a kingdom of life that is eternal; a kingdom that is built upon relationship, bonding bone to bone.

Moving on from a Firm Foundation:

When we heed Peter's advice in The Acts of the Apostles chapter two, we will have set ourselves a firm foundation, one upon which we can build securely without fear of it collapsing underneath us.

There are many who decide to ignore Peter's words who end up struggling with many difficulties, often falling by the wayside, defeated by the attacks that come from the enemy.

A building without a good foundation cannot withstand severe storms.

We however, will not only survive storms but overcome them and live in security.

The writer to the Hebrew community gives us some further advice:

So let us stop going over the basic teachings about Christ again and again.
Let us go on instead and become mature in our understanding.
Surely we don't need to start again with the fundamental importance of repenting from evil deeds and placing our faith in God.
You don't need further instruction about baptisms, the laying on of hands, the resurrection of the dead, and eternal judgement.

And so, God willing, we will move forward to further understanding.
Hebrews 6:1-3.

I get the impression that the writer was getting fed up with repeating the need to lay good foundations.

He wanted his readers to grow up, to become spiritually mature and so to establish God's kingdom as do I, but we grow according to God's pace and not by our own expectations.

The writer of this letter is not the only one who is waiting for us to reach maturity.
All of creation is waiting for us.

Paul wrote:
For all creation is waiting eagerly for that future day when God will reveal who his children really are.
Against its will, all creation was subjected to God's curse. But with eager hope, the creation looks forward to the day when it will join God's children in glorious freedom from death and decay
Romans 8:19-21.

All of creation is waiting for us, the sons and daughters, to move on from being babies: to become mature adults spiritually.

Some foundations need to be set deeper than others as they will carry greater loads.

Some may require greater flexibility or to be built taller. We are all different vessels and will grow as The Lord chooses to.

The crucial factor is a desire to know Him. If we prioritise our time with Him then we will undoubtedly grow. He knows our hearts.

We have entered a kingdom that will always be revealing new treasures: we will go from strength to strength, casting off the things that formerly restrained us, walking towards the destiny that God has already laid out ahead of us.

God has said that He has plans for us, plans for our future.

'For I know the plans I have for you," says the Lord . "They are plans for good and not for disaster, to give you a future and a hope. '
Jeremiah 29:11

Paul also, when writing to the Ephesian followers gave them this advice:

'For we are God's masterpiece. He has created us anew in Christ Jesus, so we can do the good things he planned for us long ago. '
Ephesians 2:10

God has plans for our future when we follow Him.

None of us will be given the same responsibilities, the same works, the same giftings, or the same teaching to enable us to carry out the things that God has planned for us.

We are all different, but we are working towards the same target.

We will go through different challenges, we will be tested by different things and we can support each other through our trials and testing.

It is through these things that we will become spiritually mature as we trust Him to be our provider and to supply all that we need.

We can depend upon Father to meet all of our needs in every situation.

If we trust Him entirely in truth, we will learn to depend upon Him completely and we will lose our dependency upon anything and everything that we might have thought we could supply from ourselves.

Our relationship with Jesus; with Father, will be our priority.

Raising of the Dead and Eternal Judgement:

Peter gave no advice to the crowds on the day of Pentecost with regards to eternity, what might happen when our bodies have perished or the consequence of not turning to God.

The concern was not with regards to any of those matters but what we must do now, and of life with Holy Spirit today.

It is our today and the today's of many others that Jesus was concerned also.

We are offered the opportunity to leave the kingdom of death and sin and to enter the kingdom of God today.

If we are sensible it is an offer that we need to respond to willingly and gratefully, we will be welcomed with open arms.

The writer of the letter to the Hebrews expected his readers to know about eternity and judgement.

There are some preachers today who speak of the peril of going to hell.

I have spent more time going into this misunderstanding in my book, The Thief. There we can find a whole chapter on the subject.

But very briefly here again.

My knowledge of the loving God that I am one with, does not lead me to believe He would wish to have the knowledge of souls suffering in a hell for eternity.

The realisation that we have lost the opportunity to spend an eternity with Him will be so sorrowful.

I have not found any reference to this as a place that we might be condemned to spending eternity in, anywhere in scripture, let alone any reference to suffering in eternity.

The prophet Isaiah tells us that the dead who do not know God are not raised again.

'They are now dead, they live no more; their spirits do not rise. You punished them and brought them to ruin; you wiped out all memory of them.
Isaiah 26:14.

Where the word hell is used in modern translations of scripture it is often a mistranslation of the original text or a description of the life that those who don't know God live in during the present.

Jesus once referred to hell when discussing a Hebrew folk story but there He was using Jewish folk myths to explain a parable and not reality.
Luke 16:19-26.

The terms that we read of their being, *'weeping and gnashing of teeth'*, in various places in scripture describes the sorrow of not knowing Jesus, but not one of eternal suffering.

Peter had no need to use hell in terms of a threat regarding the consequences of not acknowledging God and neither should we.

It is the love of Jesus in all that He has done for us that provokes us to want to serve Him and not the fear of death.

Fear will only produce a life of fear.

Love will produce a life filled with love. A seed can only reproduce the fruit that is similar to itself.

We who have entered the kingdom of life that Jesus has provided for us have been birthed into eternity, our bodies may fade away and die but that which is eternal within us will continue to live with Him.

Paul talks about being given a new body, which is like the body that Jesus had after His resurrection.

For we know that when this earthly tent we live in is taken down (that is, when we die and leave this earthly body), we will have a house in heaven, an eternal body made for us by God himself and not by human hands.

We grow weary in our present bodies, and we long to put on our heavenly bodies like new clothing.
For we will put on heavenly bodies; we will not be spirits without bodies.
2 Corinthians 5:1-3.

Paul gives us some more information in his first letter to the Corinthians in chapter fifteen.
I would advise anyone to read it for themselves, but he sums up by saying:

It will happen in a moment, in the blink of an eye, when the last trumpet is blown. For when the trumpet sounds, those who have died will be raised to live forever. And we who are living will also be transformed.
For our dying bodies must be transformed into bodies that will never die; our mortal bodies must be transformed into immortal bodies.
1 Corinthians 15:52-53.

The bodies that we live in at present are destined to perish and are nothing when compared with the new bodies that we will receive.

What we do whilst living within these bodies however, will have an impact on how we will spend eternity.

Our lives are a testing ground to determine what manner of person we are.

Jesus gave many indications of the principle that what we do with the gifts and abilities we are given will determine our ultimate outcome.

An example of this is the rich man who gave his servants talents:

The rich man gave different valued talents to his servants and on his return rewarded them according to their ability to increase what he had given.
Matthew 25:14-30.

To the ones who had invested their talent and had increased he gave more according to how well they had managed their responsibilities.
To those who had no return he took away what they had been given. They had not bothered to use what they had.

There are several other parables that teach the same message and so we might gather that what we do with our lives will determine the responsibilities or otherwise that we will be given when Jesus returns.

Within the book of Revelation and elsewhere there are also many indications that those who obtain victories over the trials and temptations that we face will be awarded 'crowns' or rewards, of different types both whilst in these bodies and after Jesus returns.

We are often referred to as overcomers in scripture as that is the nature that we have been given. It is a way of life that we will grow into.

Can we be trusted with finances? We may possibly be given further responsibilities.

Are we gifted with hospitality? This too is a valuable gift to have when managed well.
Are we able to administer justice or to govern wisely?

Are we kind? Are we good at parenting?

There are many areas of our lives that may be accounted for.

We are stewards of all that God has given us, in terms of abilities and belongings.

We will learn to steward those things well under the guidance of Holy Spirit.

Paul's advice to the Colosian christians was:

Work willingly at whatever you do, as though you were working for the Lord rather than for people.
Remember that the Lord will give you an inheritance as your reward, and that the Master you are serving is Christ.
Colossians 3:23-24.

With regards to the judgments that the writer to the Hebrews refers to, we can know that we will be judged and found innocent as a consequence of our faith in Jesus; what He has achieved for us in His life, death and resurrection.

We will be judged in terms of an assessment of how we have spent our lives also as we have already mentioned.

We will not be judged on what we were like before we turned to God, as Jesus has paid the price for that life: those sins.
We have redemption from that past life. It has gone.

Our judgement will not be one of condemnation but one of victory.

The dead who do not know God will not rise again. Their judgement is one of eternal death.
There is nothing of eternity within them.
The prophet Isaiah tells us that they will be forgotten.

The Return of the King:

The disciples and those who followed Jesus had the expectation that Jesus would return at any time.

They prepared each other for that event.
They were living in the last days.

Each generation since has been convinced that their generation would be the one that would see Jesus.

Two thousand years later we are still waiting for the return of Jesus. We are now experiencing many of the world events that were spoken of.

We are also witnessing a monumental change in the manner society in the world lives, with a progressive denial of God.

We are seeing the church institutions becoming more dependent upon finance and less on Jesus.
We see scandal after scandal amongst its members.
We hear false teachings from the leadership.

We can also see, at the same time, many outbreaks of the movements of God throughout the world.

People are being miraculously healed from impossible illnesses.
Drug lords are coming to Jesus, whole gangs are being changed for good.

Life destroying addictions are being removed.
The dead are being raised.
Third world orphans are being miraculously fed from nothing.

There is a thirst for spiritual matters: for something outside of themselves: a spiritual reality.

The true children of God are learning to worship Him in Spirit and in truth.
We can see God's kingdom becoming manifested.

There are opposing forces rising in the earth.

The world needs to see Jesus.

This next generation may well be the one that welcomes Him.

How will the world see Jesus?

Peter's instructions for us are foundation stones that lead us into new life with Jesus.

The writer to the Hebrew christians urges us to move on from those foundations to reach a maturity.

Paul writes that the whole earth is groaning, waiting for the sons and daughters of God to be revealed.

Jesus came to earth in order to bring restoration to a fallen world.

Our restoration to Him is a major part of that greater restoration but it is not the full restoration.

Ultimately Jesus came to redeem the world.

We each have a crucial part to play in that restoration. Each one of us are unique and our part can not be fulfilled by anyone else.

The truth is that unless we are able to fulfil our part there will be areas that are not complete.

Each one of us has a part to play in God's restoration of the world.

We have seen that a part of that restoration involves His family becoming one family in truth.

Jesus constantly prayed that we might be one in the same way that He is one with Father; that we might also become one with Him.

Our unity is an ongoing work that we will learn to build upon as we build our lives with others in faith for that to be so.

Jesus gave us an indication of how some of the situations would be when He would return and one of them is that the good news of the kingdom would be preached, or displayed, in the whole earth.

And the Good News about the Kingdom will be preached throughout the whole world, so that all nations will hear it; and then the end will come. '
Matthew 24:14.

There are many who claim that the good news has been preached throughout the earth already and that all know of Jesus, but the truth is that God's kingdom is not yet displayed on the earth.

Whilst there are many who know of Jesus, we do not see an overwhelming outworking of God's kingdom yet.

There are many schisms and divisions amongst us and little love displayed.

Jesus preached that God's kingdom is within us.

One day the Pharisees asked Jesus, "When will the Kingdom of God come?" Jesus replied, "The Kingdom of God can't be detected by visible signs.
'You won't be able to say, 'Here it is!' or 'It's over there!' For the Kingdom of God is already among you. " '
Luke 17:20-21.

God's kingdom exists within us and is displayed by our lives lived in love with each other.

Jesus, and later His disciples, taught how His life within us is outworked.

We can see for ourselves that there is some work to be done with us before we are able to see that community of God's family on the earth.

Each one of us will have different battles to face and to overcome.
Each one of us will be trained by Father, through hearing His voice for ourselves.

We are each of us, unique.

We are very immature in our faith and in the love that we might show towards others, but there are pockets of the beginnings everywhere.

In our own hearts there is a fire, a passion, to persevere and to win.

We must press on into that maturity in order to see Jesus appear amongst us.

As we play our part towards that goal we will see God's hand of acceleration in all that He is accomplishing in the earth with us.

Will we be amongst those who enable Jesus' return?

Reflecting Jesus to the world:

When Jesus returns He will be appearing as a bridegroom might meet a bride.

Let us be glad and rejoice,
and let us give honour to him.
For the time has come for the wedding feast of the Lamb,
and his bride has prepared herself.
Revelation 19:7.

We are that bride.

Our duty is to prepare ourselves for the groom's pleasure.

The groom does not prepare the bride but she prepares herself for Him.

We need to use our abilities, our gifts: the faith that we have been given, towards that end.

Our work on earth has to do with preparing ourselves to meet the groom.

As individuals, and as we become one in true unity with others we will learn to overcome the enemy in all of the ways in which he attempts to destroy the work of God.

We will see addictions removed, lives changed, mental problems resolved, incurable illnesses dispatched, miracles will be experienced, the works that Jesus carried out will be our way of life as we walk in harmony with Father, as Jesus did.

The bride will learn to take on many responsibilities as a good administrator of the kingdom.

As we learn to overcome the trials and difficulties that we face, we are being trained; we are changing, taking on the likeness of Jesus.

We are losing our former life and we are taking on His life.
It can be a painful experience at times but it is a good exchange.

As we learn to let go of all the things that we previously loved and worshipped in exchange for His life we undergo changes in our thought processes, changes in our motivations and so in our words and actions.

We begin to take on the likeness and character of Jesus.

We become less self centred and more charitable, loving; putting others needs before our own.

Looking to secure the best outcome for those we love instead of fearing for our own welfare.

This is the reason that those followers in Antioch were called christians or christ - ones.

This is the manner in which the world will see Jesus amongst us.

They will look at the bride, who is preparing herself, and see Jesus reflected in her.

It is then that the world will see God's kingdom on the earth.

It is then that Jesus will appear on the earth, among us.

This is the good news that will be preached throughout the earth.

It is towards this end that we are working.

We each have a part to play towards this outcome.
We have been summoned for this purpose.

Meeting with one another:

We have touched briefly on how the early followers of Jesus met in their homes daily, learning from the disciples teaching and enjoying meals together.

This might raise a question as to when and how do we meet up?

What is the purpose of our meeting and what do our gatherings involve?

We have left behind our old lives and are beginning a new life in fellowship with others who love Jesus.

The truth is that we will meet as often as we have something that we want to share with others.

There are no specific days or times that are to be set aside for meeting together. All of time belongs to God and we are His.

There are no designated places to meet either. I believe that the home is where we feel most comfortable and it is where we can share our lives best.

The purpose of our meeting together is to share the life that is being poured into us.

If we have been born again we will have God's Spirit within us, giving us revelation and new understanding to share with others all of the time. There is no end to the things that God wants to bring into our understanding: into our lives.

New doors will be opening to us, there will be trials and joys to share, difficulties to overcome together and blessings to enjoy.

Our new life will be an adventure shared with others.

Paul wrote various letters to the Corinthian christians and others about our meeting together.

He indicated how we should behave, putting others before ourselves, listening to Holy Spirit and being disciplined about our excitement in sharing our gifts.

All manner of teaching is available to us, we can receive revelation by reading the scriptures, by listening to teaching, by hearing what Holy Spirit is showing us in our daily lives with Him, but hearing from Father and the praise of Jesus, ensuring that Jesus is the focus of our times together and not ourselves, is something to bear in mind.

Paul wrote thus:

Well, my brothers and sisters, let's summarise.
When you meet together, one will sing, another will teach, another will tell some special revelation God has

given, one will speak in tongues, and another will interpret what is said.
But everything that is done must strengthen all of you.

No more than two or three should speak in tongues. They must speak one at a time, and someone must interpret what they say.
But if no one is present who can interpret, they must be silent in your church meeting and speak in tongues to God privately.
Let two or three people prophesy, and let the others evaluate what is said.
But if someone is prophesying and another person receives a revelation from the Lord, the one who is speaking must stop.
In this way, all who prophesy will have a turn to speak, one after the other, so that everyone will learn and be encouraged.
Remember that people who prophesy are in control of their spirit and can take turns.
For God is not a God of disorder but of peace, as in all the meetings of God's holy people.
1 Corinthians 14:26-33.

The christians in Corinth had no problem with using the spiritual gifts that they had been given, they were all eager to get involved, but apparently there was some disorder amongst them which required attention.

There will be other occasions when we simply meet up, possibly in one's or two's to build relationships to get to know each other better.

Some might describe these times as social events rather than spiritual but in truth we are one in God at all times, we reflect Him wherever we are and whatever we are doing, dependent upon our closeness to Him.

Whether we are gathering for a specific purpose or whether we are going for a meal or a walk together we are with God and His life is amongst us.

We need not make a distinction in the areas that we meet or the reasons that we meet. God is in everything we do.

We can see in the life and ministry of Jesus that He had no care of where He was. He would be as happy performing a miracle in the street or at a wedding as in a synagogue or in the temple.

His only concern was in doing what Father was telling Him to do or say.

The disciples that learnt from Him had the same experience and so should we.

The kingdom of God will not be established on the earth by many of us meeting up in large numbers, or by the use of spiritual giftings but the flesh and blood of the kingdom is built upon solid relationships.

It is out of relationship that the life of Jesus is able to flow through His body; us, who are members of His family, and then out into the world.

Meeting up outside of relationship will be a cold and stilted, legalistic situation.

God is love and where there is no love flowing there remains only legality, ritual and dogma which is unable to produce life.

So we can see that the priority for us is to build relationships with those who also love the Lord.

From those relationships will flow the life that we can share with each other and with those who need to know Jesus too.

It is in this manner that we will grow together in love, in the knowledge of Jesus, in strength through our unity, in order to overthrow the works of the enemy so that the world will see Jesus.

Today those living outside of Jesus are desperately in need of hope, security and truth.

We are able to offer the hope, security, truth and life that can be found nowhere else.

This is the reason we have been called into His Kingdom.

This is the reason that Jesus encouraged His disciples and us, to pray towards God's kingdom being established on earth.

We may be familiar with the words of Jesus when He was teaching His disciples with regards to prayer:

'May your will be done, may your kingdom come.
May your authority be established on earth in the same way that it is in heaven'.
Matthew 6:10.

It is towards this end that we continue to work to overcome all that stands in the way of God's will.

Are we standing at the edge of the age that will see these things come to pass?

It is in order to bring about a full and complete restoration of all things that Jesus gave His life and overcame death.

Whilst still on the cross Jesus declared, 'It is finished!

Jesus has accomplished all that He set out to achieve.

We are the ones who will bring that work to completion.

Will we be a part of that unstoppable momentum?

There can be no doubt that God's will cannot be thwarted.

Let us get involved with all He is doing to bring that to pass now.

There are always further questions and enquiries to be made in the Christian life – everything is new!

There is always something to discover – something to share with others.

Please feel free to email me if you have any questions, or would like to talk about this book.

To contact Tim - the author:
email: warwickhouse@mail.com

Available from Amazon worldwide and all good bookshops.

Tim has also written:
Paperback and eBooks:

Journey Into Life:

What did Jesus really preach about when He was on earth?
Within A Journey into Life we discover the joy of travelling to a new place.

Tim has set our search for God's Kingdom in the form of a journey to a new land.

Once inside the new land we begin a journey of discovery – everything is new.

Did Jesus teach that His Kingdom is within our grasp?

Is this a land – A Kingdom that we can live in now – in our own lifetime?

The answer is yes!

Some Adjustments Required?:

We live our lives from day to day carrying out regular routines and rituals often without thinking about what we do and what we say and why.

We take for granted that the things that we have done and said and even for centuries past must be correct because that is simply the way things are.

Tim has taken some of the many misunderstood concepts in the Christian life that we have, for so long, taken for granted and brought correction and redirection.

God is doing a new thing in this season and those who want to follow His direction need to hear Him.

A Time To Consider:

A Time to consider was written at a time when several friends and friends of friends had been taken Ill by potentially life threatening illnesses.

When this happens to us out of the blue it is naturally a shocking discovery to realise that we aren't going to live on this earth, in this body, forever.

It is however a reality that we all need to take into consideration.

Any of us may be taken away at any time.
Our life on earth is a very short period when we consider eternity.

Let us get involved with eternity now - we may not get another opportunity to do so.

The Shaking:

We live in a changing era.
God is moving and the earth is being shaken.
The church age is passing.
God's Kingdom age is upon us.
How do the times that we live fit with God's plan for us in eternity?
Has our own past affected our present and will it affect our future?
Can we make an impact in our time?

Our Foundations:

Many of us have missed out on vital foundational truths in our walk with the Lord.
Consequently we tend to wander around unaware that we may be missing out on the good things that Father has planned for us, unsure of where we should be or what our purpose is here on earth.
As we look into "Our Foundations" some much needed clarity and understanding will be gleaned for our benefit and for that of the emerging Kingdom.

Genesis Part One:

There are many apparent mysteries for us to uncover when reading the book of Genesis.
In Genesis part one we attempt to uncover and give an answer to some of these mysteries.
We also invite the reader to consider the text for themselves and to appreciate that the Lord is wanting us to open up a discussion with Him.

Genesis Part Two:

In Genesis part two we continue to look at the line of progression that began with Adam and will continue to the birth of Jesus.
Noah has journeyed into a new era. Life has continued as the Lord promised.
Abraham, the man of faith and the father of all who choose to trust in Jesus, is born.
The nations begin to emerge from the mists.

Genesis Part Three:

Genesis part three brings us to the birth of Isaac who is a type of Jesus.
From Isaac, through Jacob, to Joseph and into the land of Egypt we can journey with the patriarchs and the children of the man who becomes Israel.

The Lord is bringing His plan of redemption to pass.

The End Times - for those who don't know Jesus:

The End Times - for those who don't know Jesus, gives an explanation, in a relatively short book, of the times that we are living in now and the part that they have to play at the end of this age.

Entering Eternity Today:

Do we go to Heaven when we die?

For over two thousand years there has been some considerable misunderstanding and confusion with regards to God's Kingdom.

Where it is taught, the question is inevitably raised, what is God's Kingdom?
Is it a place we go to when we die?

Will we be taken there one day?
The answer to that one is a definite, no.

The enemy has been allowed to introduce an abundance of misleading teaching into the church circles that many of us inhabit in order to ensure that his kingdom remains.

When we uncover the truth of this deception and learn to live in God's promises he will flee like never before and the world will encounter a harvest unlike any other.

The Thief:

The basic beliefs and understandings of Christians are grounded in the interpretation of the scriptures that have been carried out by well meaning theologians.

But what happens to those basic foundations of truth when we discover that perhaps not all of those translations have been well made?

How great a part has the enemy of our faith played in the interpretation and representation of the scriptures that we read everyday in our bibles?

We may find that we are living at a time when our understanding of scripture requires some adjustment if we are to enter into all that Father has in store for us.

An Introduction to Jesus:

An Introduction to Jesus is a brief outline of the life of Jesus.

Including resources from all four gospels, the life of Jesus has been carefully pieced together, giving an insight into the sequence of events as they occurred during His time here on earth.

We are taken on a journey, from before the very beginning of time, through the birth, life, death, resurrection and ascension of Jesus and into the eternity that will never end.

Here we will find a description of who Jesus is, why He came to earth, what He achieved and how that might affect us.

We are offered an invitation to respond to all that Jesus is on our behalf; to know Him for ourselves.

The Reality of Jesus - What Next?

Following on from 'An Introduction to Jesus'.
'The Reality of Jesus - What Next'? deals with how we might respond to what we now know about all that Jesus has achieved on our behalf.
We have discovered that what we once doubted, is in truth, reality.
In the same manner that the crowd who responded to Peter's advice to them on the day of Pentecost, we might ask the question: What can we do?
Within these pages we will find very valuable advice as to what our response might be and also how we might continue following Jesus and all that involves.
What are our next steps?
Where do we fit in?
Where do we go from here?

Other recommended publications of related interest:

By John J Sweetman

Paperback and eBooks:

The Emerging Kingdom

The Book of Genesis trilogy:
Part One: The Beginnings
Part Two: Abraham and Isaac
Part Three: Jacob and Joseph

The Book of Exodus:
Part One: Leaving Captivity

Establishing the Kingdom series:

The Book of Joshua
The Book of Judges
The Book of Ruth
The Book of 1 Samuel
The Book of 2 Samuel
The Book of Esther
The Book of John
The Book of Romans
The Book of 1 Corinthians
The Book of 2 Corinthians
The Book of Ephesians
The Book of Galatians
The Book of Philippians

The Book of Colossians
The Book of Thessalonians
The Books of 1 and 2 Timothy
The Book of Titus
The Book of Philemon
The Book of Hebrews
The Books of 1 & 2 Peter
The Book of Jude
The Book of Revelation

Babylon or Jerusalem – your choice

Recommended Book by Fiona Sweetman
Paperback and eBook

Taste the Colour Smell the Number

Printed in Great Britain
by Amazon